# CALENDAR 2021

## JANUARY

| M | TU | W | TH | F | SA | SU |
|---|----|----|----|----|----|----|
| 28 | 29 | 30 | 31 | 1 | 2 | 3 |
| 4 | 5 | 6 | 7 | 8 | 9 | 10 |
| 11 | 12 | 13 | 14 | 15 | 16 | 17 |
| 18 | 19 | 20 | 21 | 22 | 23 | 24 |
| 25 | 26 | 27 | 28 | 29 | 30 | 31 |
|  |  |  |  |  |  |  |

## FEBRUARY

| M | TU | W | TH | F | SA | SU |
|---|----|----|----|----|----|----|
| 1 | 2 | 3 | 4 | 5 | 6 | 7 |
| 8 | 9 | 10 | 11 | 12 | 13 | 14 |
| 15 | 16 | 17 | 18 | 19 | 20 | 21 |
| 22 | 23 | 24 | 25 | 26 | 27 | 28 |
|  |  |  |  |  |  |  |

## MARCH

| M | TU | W | TH | F | SA | SU |
|---|----|----|----|----|----|----|
| 1 | 2 | 3 | 4 | 5 | 6 | 7 |
| 8 | 9 | 10 | 11 | 12 | 13 | 14 |
| 15 | 16 | 17 | 18 | 19 | 20 | 21 |
| 22 | 23 | 24 | 25 | 26 | 27 | 28 |
| 29 | 30 | 31 |  |  |  |  |

## APRIL

| M | TU | W | TH | F | SA | SU |
|---|----|----|----|----|----|----|
|  |  |  | 1 | 2 | 3 | 4 |
| 5 | 6 | 7 | 8 | 9 | 10 | 11 |
| 12 | 13 | 14 | 15 | 16 | 17 | 18 |
| 19 | 20 | 21 | 22 | 23 | 24 | 25 |
| 26 | 27 | 28 | 29 | 30 |  |  |
|  |  |  |  |  |  |  |

## MAY

| M | TU | W | TH | F | SA | SU |
|---|----|----|----|----|----|----|
|  |  |  |  |  | 1 | 2 |
| 3 | 4 | 5 | 6 | 7 | 8 | 9 |
| 10 | 11 | 12 | 13 | 14 | 15 | 16 |
| 17 | 18 | 19 | 20 | 21 | 22 | 23 |
| 24 | 25 | 26 | 27 | 28 | 29 | 30 |
| 31 |  |  |  |  |  |  |

## JUNE

| M | TU | W | TH | F | SA | SU |
|---|----|----|----|----|----|----|
|  | 1 | 2 | 3 | 4 | 5 | 6 |
| 7 | 8 | 9 | 10 | 11 | 12 | 13 |
| 14 | 15 | 16 | 17 | 18 | 19 | 20 |
| 21 | 22 | 23 | 24 | 25 | 26 | 27 |
| 28 | 29 | 30 |  |  |  |  |

## JULY

| M | TU | W | TH | F | SA | SU |
|---|----|----|----|----|----|----|
|  |  |  | 1 | 2 | 3 | 4 |
| 5 | 6 | 7 | 8 | 9 | 10 | 11 |
| 12 | 13 | 14 | 15 | 16 | 17 | 18 |
| 19 | 20 | 21 | 22 | 23 | 24 | 25 |
| 26 | 27 | 28 | 29 | 30 | 31 |  |
|  |  |  |  |  |  |  |

## AUGUST

| M | TU | W | TH | F | SA | SU |
|---|----|----|----|----|----|----|
|  |  |  |  |  |  | 1 |
| 2 | 3 | 4 | 5 | 6 | 7 | 8 |
| 9 | 10 | 11 | 12 | 13 | 14 | 15 |
| 16 | 17 | 18 | 19 | 20 | 21 | 22 |
| 23 | 24 | 25 | 26 | 27 | 28 | 29 |
| 30 | 31 |  |  |  |  |  |

## SEPTEMBER

| M | TU | W | TH | F | SA | SU |
|---|----|----|----|----|----|----|
|  |  | 1 | 2 | 3 | 4 | 5 |
| 6 | 7 | 8 | 9 | 10 | 11 | 12 |
| 13 | 14 | 15 | 16 | 17 | 18 | 19 |
| 20 | 21 | 22 | 23 | 24 | 25 | 26 |
| 27 | 28 | 29 | 30 |  |  |  |

## OCTOBER

| M | TU | W | TH | F | SA | SU |
|---|----|----|----|----|----|----|
|  |  |  |  | 1 | 2 | 3 |
| 4 | 5 | 6 | 7 | 8 | 9 | 10 |
| 11 | 12 | 13 | 14 | 15 | 16 | 17 |
| 18 | 19 | 20 | 21 | 22 | 23 | 24 |
| 25 | 26 | 27 | 28 | 29 | 30 | 31 |
|  |  |  |  |  |  |  |

## NOVEMBER

| M | TU | W | TH | F | SA | SU |
|---|----|----|----|----|----|----|
| 1 | 2 | 3 | 4 | 5 | 6 | 7 |
| 8 | 9 | 10 | 11 | 12 | 13 | 14 |
| 15 | 16 | 17 | 18 | 19 | 20 | 21 |
| 22 | 23 | 24 | 25 | 26 | 27 | 28 |
| 29 | 30 |  |  |  |  |  |

## DECEMBER

| M | TU | W | TH | F | SA | SU |
|---|----|----|----|----|----|----|
|  |  | 1 | 2 | 3 | 4 | 5 |
| 6 | 7 | 8 | 9 | 10 | 11 | 12 |
| 13 | 14 | 15 | 16 | 17 | 18 | 19 |
| 20 | 21 | 22 | 23 | 24 | 25 | 26 |
| 27 | 28 | 29 | 30 | 31 |  |  |
|  |  |  |  |  |  |  |

# CALENDAR 2022

## JANUARY

| M | TU | W | TH | F | SA | SU |
|---|----|----|----|----|----|----|
| 27 | 28 | 29 | 30 | 31 | 1 | 2 |
| 3 | 4 | 5 | 6 | 7 | 8 | 9 |
| 10 | 11 | 12 | 13 | 14 | 15 | 16 |
| 17 | 18 | 19 | 20 | 21 | 22 | 23 |
| 24 | 25 | 26 | 27 | 28 | 29 | 30 |
| 31 | | | | | | |

## FEBRUARY

| M | TU | W | TH | F | SA | SU |
|---|----|----|----|----|----|----|
| | 1 | 2 | 3 | 4 | 5 | 6 |
| 7 | 8 | 9 | 10 | 11 | 12 | 13 |
| 14 | 15 | 16 | 17 | 18 | 19 | 20 |
| 21 | 22 | 23 | 24 | 25 | 26 | 27 |
| 28 | | | | | | |

## MARCH

| M | TU | W | TH | F | SA | SU |
|---|----|----|----|----|----|----|
| | 1 | 2 | 3 | 4 | 5 | 6 |
| 7 | 8 | 9 | 10 | 11 | 12 | 13 |
| 14 | 15 | 16 | 17 | 18 | 19 | 20 |
| 21 | 22 | 23 | 24 | 25 | 26 | 27 |
| 28 | 29 | 30 | 31 | | | |

## APRIL

| M | TU | W | TH | F | SA | SU |
|---|----|----|----|----|----|----|
| | | | | 1 | 2 | 3 |
| 4 | 5 | 6 | 7 | 8 | 9 | 10 |
| 11 | 12 | 13 | 14 | 15 | 16 | 17 |
| 18 | 19 | 20 | 21 | 22 | 23 | 24 |
| 25 | 26 | 27 | 28 | 29 | 30 | |

## MAY

| M | TU | W | TH | F | SA | SU |
|---|----|----|----|----|----|----|
| | | | | | | 1 |
| 2 | 3 | 4 | 5 | 6 | 7 | 8 |
| 9 | 10 | 11 | 12 | 13 | 14 | 15 |
| 16 | 17 | 18 | 19 | 20 | 21 | 22 |
| 23 | 24 | 25 | 26 | 27 | 28 | 29 |
| 30 | 31 | | | | | |

## JUNE

| M | TU | W | TH | F | SA | SU |
|---|----|----|----|----|----|----|
| | | 1 | 2 | 3 | 4 | 5 |
| 6 | 7 | 8 | 9 | 10 | 11 | 12 |
| 13 | 14 | 15 | 16 | 17 | 18 | 19 |
| 20 | 21 | 22 | 23 | 24 | 25 | 26 |
| 27 | 28 | 29 | 30 | | | |

## JULY

| M | TU | W | TH | F | SA | SU |
|---|----|----|----|----|----|----|
| | | | | 1 | 2 | 3 |
| 4 | 5 | 6 | 7 | 8 | 9 | 10 |
| 11 | 12 | 13 | 14 | 15 | 16 | 17 |
| 18 | 19 | 20 | 21 | 22 | 23 | 24 |
| 25 | 26 | 27 | 28 | 29 | 30 | 31 |

## AUGUST

| M | TU | W | TH | F | SA | SU |
|---|----|----|----|----|----|----|
| 1 | 2 | 3 | 4 | 5 | 6 | 7 |
| 8 | 9 | 10 | 11 | 12 | 13 | 14 |
| 15 | 16 | 17 | 18 | 19 | 20 | 21 |
| 22 | 23 | 24 | 25 | 26 | 27 | 28 |
| 29 | 30 | 31 | | | | |

## SEPTEMBER

| M | TU | W | TH | F | SA | SU |
|---|----|----|----|----|----|----|
| | | | 1 | 2 | 3 | 4 |
| 5 | 6 | 7 | 8 | 9 | 10 | 11 |
| 12 | 13 | 14 | 15 | 16 | 17 | 18 |
| 19 | 20 | 21 | 22 | 23 | 24 | 25 |
| 26 | 27 | 28 | 29 | 30 | | |

## OCTOBER

| M | TU | W | TH | F | SA | SU |
|---|----|----|----|----|----|----|
| | | | | | 1 | 2 |
| 3 | 4 | 5 | 6 | 7 | 8 | 9 |
| 10 | 11 | 12 | 13 | 14 | 15 | 16 |
| 17 | 18 | 19 | 20 | 21 | 22 | 23 |
| 24 | 25 | 26 | 27 | 28 | 29 | 30 |
| 31 | | | | | | |

## NOVEMBER

| M | TU | W | TH | F | SA | SU |
|---|----|----|----|----|----|----|
| | 1 | 2 | 3 | 4 | 5 | 6 |
| 7 | 8 | 9 | 10 | 11 | 12 | 13 |
| 14 | 15 | 16 | 17 | 18 | 19 | 20 |
| 21 | 22 | 23 | 24 | 25 | 26 | 27 |
| 28 | 29 | 30 | | | | |

## DECEMBER

| M | TU | W | TH | F | SA | SU |
|---|----|----|----|----|----|----|
| | | | 1 | 2 | 3 | 4 |
| 5 | 6 | 7 | 8 | 9 | 10 | 11 |
| 12 | 13 | 14 | 15 | 16 | 17 | 18 |
| 19 | 20 | 21 | 22 | 23 | 24 | 25 |
| 26 | 27 | 28 | 29 | 30 | 31 | |

# HOLIDAY/RELIGIOUS OBSERVANCES

31st December – New Years Eve
1st January – New Years Day – HAPPY NEW YEAR 2021
2nd January – Extra Bank Holiday (Scot.)
20th January – Martin Luther King Jr. Day (USA)
25th January – Burns Night (Scot.)
12th February – Chinese New Year
14th February – Valentine's Day
16th/17th February – Carnival (UK)
17th February – President's Day (USA)
1st March – St. David's Day – (Wales)
14th March – Mother's Day (UK)
17th March – St. Patrick's Day (USA, UK/N.I)
28th March – British Summer Time Starts @ 2am
1st April – April Fools Day
2nd April – Good Friday
4th April – Easter Sunday
5th April – Easter Monday (Scot.)
5th April – End of Tax Year 2020 (UK)
6th April – Start of New Tax Year 2021 (UK)
15th April – Tax Day (USA)
23rd April – St. George's Day/Shakespeare Day (UK)
3rd May – May Bank Holiday (UK)
5th May – Cinco de Mayo (USA)
9th May – Mother's Day (USA)
31st May – Memorial Day (USA)
31st May – Spring Bank Holiday (UK)
12th June – Battle of the Boyne (N.I)
12th June – Queen's Birthday (UK)
20th June – Father's Day (USA/UK)
21st June – Summer Solstice
22nd June – Windrush Day

# HOLIDAY/RELIGIOUS OBSERVANCES

3rd July – 'Independence Day' observed (USA)
4th July – Independence Day (USA)
5th July – Independence Day (Observed, USA)
12th July – Battle of the Boyne (N.I)
2nd August – Summer Bank Holiday (Scotland)
30th August – Summer Bank Holiday (UK)
6th September – Labor Day (USA)
11th October – Columbus Day (USA)
31st October – British Summer Time Ends @ 2am
31st October – Halloween
31st October – Paper Tax Returns Deadline 2020
2nd November – Election Day (USA)
5th November – Guy Fawke's Day (UK)
11th November – Remembrance Sunday (UK)
11th November – Veteran's Day (USA)
14th November – Armistice Day/Remembrance Day Observed (UK)
25th November – Thanksgiving Day (USA)
26th November – Black Friday (USA)
30th November – St. Andrew's Day – (Scot.)
21st December – Winter Solstice – HAPPY YULE
24th December – Christmas Eve
25th December – Christmas Day – HAPPY CHRISTMAS
26th December – Boxing Day (UK)
27th December – Bank Holiday (UK)
28th December – Bank Holiday extra (Scot.)
31st December – New Years Eve
1st January – New Years Day – HAPPY NEW YEAR 2022

# PERSONAL MEMORANDA

NAME: _____

ADDRESS: _____

_____

_____

_____

TEL: _____

MOBILE: _____

EMAIL: _____

HOME INSURANCE NO.: _____

HOME INSURANCE DUE: _____

DRIVERS LICENCE NO.: _____

BUSINESS NAME: _____

BUSINESS WEBSITE: _____

UTR/INCOME TAX PAN: _____

TAX ASSESSMENT DATE: _____

TAX PAYABLE DATE: _____

BUSINESS INSURANCE NO.: _____

BUSINESS INSURANCE DUE: _____

INSURANCE POLICY NO.: _____

INSURANCE PREMIUM DUE: _____

# GARDEN PLANNING & PLANTING LOGS

**28 pages** of plants information for you to insert details in a log style book along with a diary for you to add your day to day routine or for other daily information.

Within these garden logs you can add the processes from seed and potting to then the process of obtaining seed through drying or hanging.

Watch and note all about your plants and in particular the weather and water amounts along with how fast they grow and even size under notes or outcome.

Think about how you would like to plan your plot or rotation of harvest and also your garden with the spare sketch paper at back of book. Keep on top of your plantings and have fun in watching them grow after all your hard effort! Green fingers with joy in your heart!

*PLUS*

**2 pages** for you to plan your garden layout and also allotment crop annual rotation so you will never forget what and where you planted the year before. Crop rotation is very important for soil nutrition. Each square is 2cm x 2cm, add size you require in feet or metres per square for your accuracy. **1 page** for plants names planted and to be planted.

---

Date:

Name of Plant:

Watering Requirements

Sunlight/Shade Requirements

☐ Seed/Pot  ☐ Transplant  ☐ Pick/Dead Head  ☐ Dry Seed/Hang

| Date | Plant Requirements ... |
| --- | --- |
|  |  |
|  |  |
|  |  |
|  |  |
|  |  |

Notes:

Outcome:

Uses:

# CONVERSION TABLES

## LENGTH

| Centimetres (cm) | CM or Inches | Inches |
|---|---|---|
| 02.54 | 1 | 0.394 |
| 05.08 | 2 | 0.787 |
| 07.62 | 3 | 1.181 |
| 10.16 | 4 | 1.575 |
| 12.70 | 5 | 1.969 |
| 15.24 | 6 | 2.362 |
| 17.78 | 7 | 2.756 |
| 20.32 | 8 | 3.150 |
| 22.86 | 9 | 3.543 |
| 25.40 | 10 | 3.937 |
| 50.80 | 20 | 7.874 |
| 76.20 | 30 | 11.811 |
| 101.60 | 40 | 15.748 |
| 127.00 | 50 | 19.685 |

| Kilometres (km) | KM or Miles | Miles |
|---|---|---|
| 01.609 | 1 | 00.621 |
| 03.219 | 2 | 01.243 |
| 04.828 | 3 | 01.864 |
| 06.437 | 4 | 02.485 |
| 08.047 | 5 | 03.107 |
| 09.656 | 6 | 03.728 |
| 11.265 | 7 | 04.350 |
| 12.875 | 8 | 04.971 |
| 14.484 | 9 | 05.592 |
| 16.093 | 10 | 06.214 |
| 32.187 | 20 | 12.427 |
| 48.280 | 30 | 18.641 |
| 64.374 | 40 | 24.855 |
| 80.467 | 50 | 31.069 |

## CAPACITY

| | | |
|---|---|---|
| 10 Millilitres | = | 1 Centilitre |
| 10 Centilitres | = | 1 Decilitre |
| 1 Litre | = | 1 Cu Decilitre |
| 10 Litres | = | 1 Decalitre |
| 10 Decalitres | = | 1 Hectolitre |
| 10 Hectolitres | = | 1 Kilolitre |
| 1 Kilolitre | = | 1 Cu Metre |

## MASS (WEIGHT)

| Kilograms | kg | Pounds |
|---|---|---|
| 0.454 | 1 | 2.205 |
| 0.907 | 2 | 4.409 |
| 1.361 | 3 | 6.614 |
| 1.814 | 4 | 8.819 |
| 2.268 | 5 | 11.023 |
| 2.722 | 6 | 13.228 |
| 3.175 | 7 | 15.432 |
| 3.629 | 8 | 17.637 |
| 4.082 | 9 | 19.842 |
| 4.536 | 10 | 22.046 |
| 9.072 | 20 | 44.092 |
| 13.608 | 30 | 66 139 |
| 18.144 | 40 | 88.185 |
| 22.680 | 50 | 110.231 |

## AREA

| Hectares | Ha or Acres | Acres |
|---|---|---|
| 4.456 | 1 | 2.471 |
| 0.809 | 2 | 4.942 |
| 1.214 | 3 | 7.413 |
| 1.619 | 4 | 9.884 |
| 2.023 | 5 | 12.884 |
| 2.428 | 6 | 14.826 |
| 2.833 | 7 | 17.297 |
| 3.237 | 8 | 19.769 |
| 3.642 | 9 | 22.240 |
| 4.047 | 10 | 24.711 |
| 8.094 | 20 | 49.421 |
| 12.140 | 30 | 74.132 |
| 16.187 | 40 | 98.842 |
| 20.234 | 50 | 123.553 |

## METRIC UNITS (AREA)

| | |
|---|---|
| 100 sq millimetres | = 1 sq centimetre |
| 100 sq centimetres | = 1 sq decimetre |
| 100 sq decimetres | = 1 sq metre |
| 100 sq metres | = 1 acre |
| 100 acres | = 1 hectare |
| 100 hectares | = 1 sq kilometre |

# CONVERSION TABLES

## CONVERSION FORMULAE

| To Convert | Multiply by |
|---|---|
| Inches to Centimetres | 2.54 |
| Centimetres to Inches | 0.393701 |
| Feet to Metres | 0.3048 |
| Metres to Feet | 3.2808 |
| Yards to Metres | 0.9144 |
| Metres to Yards | 1.09361 |
| Miles to Kilometres | 1.60934 |
| Kilometres to Miles | 0.621371 |
| Square Inches to Square Centimetres | 6.4516 |
| Square Centimetres to Square Inches | 0.155 |
| Square Metres to Square Feet | 10.7639 |
| Square Feet to Square Metres | 0.092903 |
| Square Yards to Square Metres | 0.836127 |
| Square Metres to Square Yards | 1.19599 |
| Square Miles to Square Kilometres | 2.58999 |
| Square Kilometres to Square Miles | 0.386103 |
| Acres to Hectares | 0.404678 |
| Hectares to Acres | 2.47101 |
| Cubic Inches to Cubic Centimetres | 16.3871 |
| Cubic Centimetres to Cubic Inches | 0.0610237 |
| Cubic Feet to Cubic Metres | 0.0283168 |
| Cubic Metres to Cubic Feet | 35.3147 |
| Cubic Yards to Cubic Metres | 0.764555 |
| Cubic Metres to Cubic Yards | 1.30795 |
| Cubic Inches to Litres | 0.016387 |
| Litres to Cubic Inches | 61.024 |
| Gallons to Litres | 4.546 |
| Litres to Gallons | 0.22 |
| Grains to Grams | 0.0648 |
| Grams to Grains | 15.43 |
| Ounces to Grams | 28.3495 |
| Grams to Ounces | 0.35274 |
| Pounds to Grams | 453.592 |
| Grams to Pounds | 0.00220462 |
| Pounds to Kilograms | 0.4536 |
| Kilograms to Pounds | 2.20462 |
| Tons to Kilograms | 1016.05 |
| Kilograms to Tons | 0.0009842 |
| 1 International Nautical Mile | 1852 Metres |

# JANUARY

| M | TU | W | TH | F | SA | SU |
|---|----|----|----|----|----|----|
| 28 | 29 | 30 | 31 | 1 | 2 | 3 |
| 4 | 5 | 6 | 7 | 8 | 9 | 10 |
| 11 | 12 | 13 | 14 | 15 | 16 | 17 |
| 18 | 19 | 20 | 21 | 22 | 23 | 24 |
| 25 | 26 | 27 | 28 | 29 | 30 | 31 |

**CELEBRATIONS/BIRTHDAYS ETC.:**

| TASKS | IMPORTANT DATES |
|---|---|
|  |  |
|  |  |
|  |  |
|  |  |
|  |  |
|  |  |
|  |  |
|  |  |
|  |  |
|  | ⬤ NEW MOON: 13TH JANUARY 2021 |
|  | ◯ FULL MOON: 28TH JANUARY 2021 |
|  | ECLIPSE/SUPERMOON/METEORS |
|  |  |

## NOTES

|  |
|---|
|  |
|  |
|  |
|  |
|  |
|  |
|  |
|  |
|  |
|  |
|  |
|  |
|  |
|  |
|  |
|  |

# JANUARY 4TH ~ 10TH JANUARY 2021

## IMPORTANT DATES & OBSERVANCES

4TH JANUARY ~ SUBSTITUTE DAY (SCOT.)
6TH JANUARY ~ EPIPHANY
7TH JANUARY ~ ORTHODOX CHRISTMAS DAY

## MONDAY

## TUESDAY

## WEDNESDAY

## THURSDAY

## FRIDAY

## SATURDAY

## SUNDAY

# DECEMBER 28TH 2020 ~ 3RD JANUARY 2021

## IMPORTANT DATES & OBSERVANCES

28TH DECEMBER ~ BOXING DAY (SUBSTITUTE DAY) (UK)
31ST DECEMBER ~ NEW YEARS EVE
1ST JANUARY ~ NEW YEARS DAY

### MONDAY

### TUESDAY

### WEDNESDAY

## THURSDAY

## FRIDAY

## SATURDAY

## SUNDAY

# JANUARY 11TH ~ 17TH JANUARY 2021

## IMPORTANT DATES & OBSERVANCES

14TH JANUARY ~ ORTHODOX NEW YEAR

## MONDAY

## TUESDAY

## WEDNESDAY

## THURSDAY

## FRIDAY

## SATURDAY

## SUNDAY

# JANUARY 18TH ~ 24TH JANUARY 2021
## IMPORTANT DATES & OBSERVANCES
18TH JANUARY ~ MARTIN LUTHER KING JR. DAY (USA)

## MONDAY

## TUESDAY

## WEDNESDAY

## THURSDAY

## FRIDAY

## SATURDAY

## SUNDAY

# JANUARY 25TH ~ 31ST JANUARY 2021
## IMPORTANT DATES & OBSERVANCES

25TH JANUARY ~ BURNS NIGHT (SCOT.)
28TH JANUARY ~ TU B'SHEVAT (ARBOR DAY)
31ST JANUARY ~ LAST DAY FOR TAX RETURNS (UK)

## MONDAY

## TUESDAY

## WEDNESDAY

## THURSDAY

## FRIDAY

## SATURDAY

## SUNDAY

# FEBRUARY

| M | TU | W | TH | F | SA | SU |
|---|----|----|----|----|----|----|
| 1 | 2 | 3 | 4 | 5 | 6 | 7 |
| 8 | 9 | 10 | 11 | 12 | 13 | 14 |
| 15 | 16 | 17 | 18 | 19 | 20 | 21 |
| 22 | 23 | 24 | 25 | 26 | 27 | 28 |
| | | | | | | |
| | | | | | | |

## CELEBRATIONS/BIRTHDAYS ETC.:

## TASKS

## IMPORTANT DATES

⬤ NEW MOON:  11TH FEBRUARY 2021

◯ FULL MOON:  27TH FEBUARY 2021

ECLIPSE/SUPERMOON/METEORS

## NOTES

# FEBRUARY 1ST ~ 7TH FEBRUARY 2021

## IMPORTANT DATES & OBSERVANCES

1ST FEBRUARY ~ NATIONAL FREEDOM DAY (USA)
2ND FEBRUARY ~ GROUNDHOG DAY (USA)
5TH FEBRUARY ~ NATIONAL WEAR RED DAY (USA)

**MONDAY**

**TUESDAY**

**WEDNESDAY**

## THURSDAY

## FRIDAY

## SATURDAY

## SUNDAY

# FEBRUARY 8TH ~ 14TH FEBRUARY 2021

## IMPORTANT DATES & OBSERVANCES

12TH FEBRUARY ~ LINCOLN'S BIRTHDAY (USA)
12TH FEBRUARY ~ CHINESE NEW YEAR
14TH FEBRUARY ~ VALENTINES DAY

## MONDAY

## TUESDAY

## WEDNESDAY

## THURSDAY

## FRIDAY

## SATURDAY

## SUNDAY

# FEBRUARY 15TH ~ 21ST FEBRUARY 2021
## IMPORTANT DATES & OBSERVANCES

15TH FEBRUARY ~ PRESIDENT'S DAY (USA)
16TH & 17TH FEBRUARY ~ CARNIVAL (UK)
16TH FEBRUARY ~ SHROVE TUESDAY
16TH FEBRUARY ~ MARDI GRAS (USA)
17TH FEBRUARY ~ ASH WEDNESDAY - LENT

## MONDAY

## TUESDAY

## WEDNESDAY

## THURSDAY

## FRIDAY

## SATURDAY

## SUNDAY

# FEBRUARY 22ND ~ 28TH FEBRUARY 2021

## IMPORTANT DATES & OBSERVANCES

26TH FEBRUARY ~ PURIM (UK)
27TH FEBRUARY ~ PURIM (USA)

## MONDAY

## TUESDAY

## WEDNESDAY

## THURSDAY

## FRIDAY

## SATURDAY

## SUNDAY

# MARCH

| M | TU | W | TH | F | SA | SU |
|---|----|----|----|----|----|----|
| 1 | 2 | 3 | 4 | 5 | 6 | 7 |
| 8 | 9 | 10 | 11 | 12 | 13 | 14 |
| 15 | 16 | 17 | 18 | 19 | 20 | 21 |
| 22 | 23 | 24 | 25 | 26 | 27 | 28 |
| 29 | 30 | 31 | | | | |

## CELEBRATIONS/BIRTHDAYS ETC.:

| TASKS | IMPORTANT DATES |
|---|---|
| | |
| | |
| | |
| | |
| | |
| | |
| | |
| | |
| | |
| | |
| | |
| | |
| | |
| | |

● NEW MOON:  13TH MARCH 2021

○ FULL MOON:  28TH MARCH 2021

ECLIPSE/SUPERMOON/METEORS

## NOTES

# MARCH 1ST ~ 7TH MARCH 2021

## IMPORTANT DATES & OBSERVANCES

1ST MARCH ~ ST. DAVID'S DAY (UK)
2ND MARCH ~ READ ACROSS AMERICA DAY (USA)
5TH MARCH ~ EMPLOYEE APPRECIATION DAY (USA)

## MONDAY

## TUESDAY

## WEDNESDAY

## THURSDAY

## FRIDAY

## SATURDAY

## SUNDAY

# MARCH 8TH ~ 14TH MARCH 2021
## IMPORTANT DATES & OBSERVANCES

11TH MARCH ~ MAHA SHIVRATRI
11TH MARCH ~ ISRA AND MI'RAJ
14TH MARCH ~ MOTHERS' DAY (UK)
14TH MARCH ~ DAYLIGHT SAVINGS TIME BEGINS (USA)

## MONDAY

## TUESDAY

## WEDNESDAY

## THURSDAY

## FRIDAY

## SATURDAY

## SUNDAY

# MARCH 15TH ~ 21ST MARCH 2021

## IMPORTANT DATES & OBSERVANCES

17TH MARCH ~ ST. PATRICK'S DAY
20TH MARCH ~ SPRING EQUINOX

## MONDAY

## TUESDAY

## WEDNESDAY

## THURSDAY

## FRIDAY

## SATURDAY

## SUNDAY

# MARCH 22ND ~ 28TH MARCH 2021
## IMPORTANT DATES & OBSERVANCES

28TH MARCH ~ PASSOVER STARTS
28TH MARCH ~ DAYLIGHT SAVINGS TIME STARTS (UK)
28TH MARCH ~ PALM SUNDAY

## MONDAY

## TUESDAY

## WEDNESDAY

67 today yippee
(i don't think)

## THURSDAY

## FRIDAY

## SATURDAY

planted rubeckia seeds in greenhouse, finished moving all the plum tree branches from allotment

## SUNDAY

planted Lupin seeds

# APRIL

| M | TU | W | TH | F | SA | SU |
|---|----|---|----|---|----|----|
|   |    |   | 1 | 2 | 3 | 4 |
| 5 | 6 | 7 | 8 | 9 | 10 | 11 |
| 12 | 13 | 14 | 15 | 16 | 17 | 18 |
| 19 | 20 | 21 | 22 | 23 | 24 | 25 |
| 26 | 27 | 28 | 29 | 30 |   |   |

## CELEBRATIONS/BIRTHDAYS ETC.:

## TASKS

## IMPORTANT DATES

NEW MOON:  12TH APRIL 2021

FULL MOON:  27TH APRIL 2021

ECLIPSE/SUPERMOON/METEORS

## NOTES

# MARCH 29TH ~ 4TH APRIL 2021

## IMPORTANT DATES & OBSERVANCES

29TH MARCH ~ HOLI
1ST APRIL ~ APRIL FOOLS' DAY
1ST APRIL ~ MAUNDY THURSDAY
2ND APRIL ~ GOOD FRIDAY
3RD APRIL ~ HOLY SATURDAY
4TH APRIL ~ EASTER DAY
4TH APRIL ~ LAST DAY OF PASSOVER

## MONDAY

Mal·o birthday

## TUESDAY

## WEDNESDAY

## THURSDAY

## FRIDAY

## SATURDAY

## SUNDAY

# APRIL 5TH ~ 11TH APRIL 2021

## IMPORTANT DATES & OBSERVANCES

5TH APRIL ~ EASTER MONDAY
8TH APRIL ~ YOM HASHOAH
5TH APRIL ~ LAST DAY OF TAX YEAR 2020 (UK)
6TH APRIL ~ FIRST DAY OF TAX YEAR 2021 (UK)

## MONDAY

## TUESDAY

## WEDNESDAY

## THURSDAY

## FRIDAY

## SATURDAY

planted 1 row beetroot
" 4 rows onions

## SUNDAY

# APRIL 12TH ~ 10TH APRIL 2021

## IMPORTANT DATES & OBSERVANCES

13TH APRIL ~ RAMADAN STARTS
13TH APRIL ~ NATIONAL LIBRARY WORKERS DAY (USA)
13TH APRIL ~ THOMAS JEFFERSON BIRTHDAY (USA)
15TH APRIL ~ TAX DAY (USA)
15TH APRIL ~ YOM HAATZMAUT

## MONDAY

## TUESDAY

## WEDNESDAY

planted 2 rows of taties

## THURSDAY

## FRIDAY

## SATURDAY

## SUNDAY

# APRIL 19TH ~ 25TH APRIL 2021
## IMPORTANT DATES & OBSERVANCES

21ST APRIL ~ ADMINISTRATIVE PROFESSIONALS DAY (USA)
22ND APRIL ~ TAKE OUR SONS AND DAUGHTERS TO WORK DAY (USA)
22ND APRIL ~ STEPHEN LAWRENCE DAY (UK)
22ND APRIL ~ EARTH DAY
23RD APRIL ~ ST. GEORGE'S DAY (UK)
23RD APRIL ~ SHAKESPEARE DAY (UK)

## MONDAY

## TUESDAY

## WEDNESDAY

## THURSDAY

## FRIDAY

## SATURDAY

## SUNDAY

# APRIL 26TH ~ 2ND MAY 2021
## IMPORTANT DATES & OBSERVANCES

30TH APRIL ~ LAG B'OMER
30TH APRIL ~ ORTHODOX GOOD FRIDAY
30TH APRIL ~ ARBOR DAY (USA)
1ST MAY ~ MAY DAY
2ND MAY ~ ORTHODOX EASTER

## MONDAY

## TUESDAY

## WEDNESDAY

## THURSDAY

## FRIDAY

## SATURDAY

## SUNDAY

# MAY

| M | TU | W | TH | F | SA | SU |
|---|---|---|---|---|---|---|
|  |  |  |  |  | 1 | 2 |
| 3 | 4 | 5 | 6 | 7 | 8 | 9 |
| 10 | 11 | 12 | 13 | 14 | 15 | 16 |
| 17 | 18 | 19 | 20 | 21 | 22 | 23 |
| 24 | 25 | 26 | 27 | 28 | 29 | 30 |
| 31 |  |  |  |  |  |  |

## CELEBRATIONS/BIRTHDAYS ETC.:

| TASKS | IMPORTANT DATES |
|---|---|
| | |
| | |
| | |
| | |
| | |
| | |
| | |
| | |
| | |
| | |
| | |
| | ● NEW MOON:  11TH MAY 2021 |
| | ○ FULL MOON:  26TH MAY 2021 |
| | ECLIPSE/SUPERMOON/METEORS |
| | 26TH MAY: TOTAL  LUNAR ECLIPSE |

## NOTES

| |
|---|
| |
| |
| |
| |
| |
| |
| |
| |
| |
| |
| |
| |
| |
| |
| |
| |
| |

# MAY 3RD ~ 9TH MAY 2021
## IMPORTANT DATES & OBSERVANCES

3RD MAY ~ EARLY BANK HOLIDAY (UK)
5TH MAY ~ CINCO DE MAYO (USA)
6TH MAY ~ NATIONAL NURSES DAY (USA)
6TH MAY ~ NATIONAL DAY OF PRAYER (USA)
8TH MAY ~ LAYLAT AL QADR (NIGHT OF POWER)
9TH MAY ~ MOTHER'S DAY (USA)

## MONDAY

## TUESDAY

## WEDNESDAY

## THURSDAY

## FRIDAY

## SATURDAY

## SUNDAY

# MAY 10TH ~ 16TH MAY 2021
## IMPORTANT DATES & OBSERVANCES

13TH MAY ~ EID AL FITR
13TH MAY ~ ASCENSION DAY
15TH MAY ~ PEACE OFFICERS MEMORIAL DAY (USA)
15TH MAY ~ ARMED FORCES DAY (USA)

## MONDAY

## TUESDAY

## WEDNESDAY

## THURSDAY

## FRIDAY

## SATURDAY

## SUNDAY

# MAY 17TH ~ 23RD MAY 2021

## IMPORTANT DATES & OBSERVANCES

17TH MAY ~ SHAVUOT
22ND MAY ~ NATIONAL MARITIME DAY (USA)
23RD MAY ~ PENTECOST

## MONDAY

## TUESDAY

## WEDNESDAY

## THURSDAY

## FRIDAY

## SATURDAY

## SUNDAY

# MAY 24TH ~ 30TH MAY 2021

## IMPORTANT DATES & OBSERVANCES

24TH MAY ~ WHIT MONDAY
30TH MAY ~ TRINITY SUNDAY

## MONDAY

## TUESDAY

## WEDNESDAY

## THURSDAY

## FRIDAY

## SATURDAY

## SUNDAY

# JUNE

| M | TU | W | TH | F | SA | SU |
|---|----|----|----|----|----|----|
|   | 1 | 2 | 3 | 4 | 5 | 6 |
| 7 | 8 | 9 | 10 | 11 | 12 | 13 |
| 14 | 15 | 16 | 17 | 18 | 19 | 20 |
| 21 | 22 | 23 | 24 | 25 | 26 | 27 |
| 28 | 29 | 30 |   |   |   |   |

## CELEBRATIONS/BIRTHDAYS ETC.:

| TASKS | IMPORTANT DATES |
|---|---|
| | |
| | |
| | |
| | |
| | |
| | |
| | |
| | |
| | |
| | |
| | ⚫ NEW MOON: 10TH JUNE 2021 |
| | ⚪ FULL MOON: 24TH JUNE 2021 |
| | ECLIPSE/SUPERMOON/METEORS |
| | 10TH JUNE: ANNULAR SOLAR ECLIPSE |

## NOTES

# MAY 31ST ~ 6TH JUNE 2021
## IMPORTANT DATES & OBSERVANCES

31ST MAY ~ MEMORIAL DAY (USA)
31ST MAY ~ SPRING BANK HOLIDAY (UK)
3RD JUNE ~ CORPUS CHRISTI
6TH JUNE ~ D-DAY

## MONDAY

## TUESDAY

## WEDNESDAY

## THURSDAY

## FRIDAY

## SATURDAY

## SUNDAY

# JUNE 7TH ~ 13TH JUNE 2021
## IMPORTANT DATES & OBSERVANCES

11TH JUNE ~ RATH YATRA
12TH JUNE ~ THE QUEEN'S BIRTHDAY (UK)

## MONDAY

## TUESDAY

## WEDNESDAY

## THURSDAY

## FRIDAY

## SATURDAY

## SUNDAY

# JUNE 14TH ~ 20TH JUNE 2021

## IMPORTANT DATES & OBSERVANCES

14TH JUNE ~ FLAG DAY (USA)
20TH JUNE ~ FATHERS' DAY
20TH JUNE ~ SUMMER SOLSTICE (USA)

## MONDAY

## TUESDAY

## WEDNESDAY

## THURSDAY

## FRIDAY

## SATURDAY

## SUNDAY

# JUNE 21ST ~ 27TH JUNE 2021
## IMPORTANT DATES & OBSERVANCES
21ST JUNE ~ SUMMER SOLSTICE
22ND JUNE ~ WINDRUSH DAY (UK)

**MONDAY**

**TUESDAY**

**WEDNESDAY**

## THURSDAY

## FRIDAY

## SATURDAY

## SUNDAY

# JULY

| M | TU | W | TH | F | SA | SU |
|---|----|----|----|----|----|----|
|  |  |  | 1 | 2 | 3 | 4 |
| 5 | 6 | 7 | 8 | 9 | 10 | 11 |
| 12 | 13 | 14 | 15 | 16 | 17 | 18 |
| 19 | 20 | 21 | 22 | 23 | 24 | 25 |
| 26 | 27 | 28 | 29 | 30 | 31 |  |

## CELEBRATIONS/BIRTHDAYS ETC.:

## TASKS

## IMPORTANT DATES

**NEW MOON:** 10TH JULY 2021

**FULL MOON:** 24TH JULY 2021

ECLIPSE/SUPERMOON/METEORS

## NOTES

# JUNE 28TH ~ 4TH JULY 2021
## IMPORTANT DATES & OBSERVANCES
4TH JULY ~ INDEPENDANCE DAY (USA)

## MONDAY

## TUESDAY

## WEDNESDAY

## THURSDAY

## FRIDAY

## SATURDAY

## SUNDAY

# JULY 5TH ~ 11TH JULY 2021
## IMPORTANT DATES & OBSERVANCES

5TH JULY~ INDEPENDANCE DAY OBSERVED (USA)

## MONDAY

## TUESDAY

## WEDNESDAY

## THURSDAY

## FRIDAY

## SATURDAY

## SUNDAY

# JULY 12TH ~ 18TH JULY 2021

## IMPORTANT DATES & OBSERVANCES

12TH JULY ~ BATTLE OF THE BOYNE (N.I)
18TH JULY ~ TISHA B'AV
19TH JULY ~ DAY OF ARAFAT

## MONDAY

## TUESDAY

## WEDNESDAY

## THURSDAY

## FRIDAY

## SATURDAY

## SUNDAY

# JULY 19TH ~ 25TH JULY 2021

## IMPORTANT DATES & OBSERVANCES

20TH JULY ~ EID AL ADHA
25TH JULY ~ PARENTS DAY (USA)

### MONDAY

### TUESDAY

### WEDNESDAY

## THURSDAY

## FRIDAY

## SATURDAY

## SUNDAY

# JULY 26TH ~ 1ST AUGUST 2021

## IMPORTANT DATES & OBSERVANCES

1ST AUGUST ~ FRIENDSHIP DAY (USA)

## MONDAY

## TUESDAY

## WEDNESDAY

## THURSDAY

## FRIDAY

## SATURDAY

## SUNDAY

# AUGUST

| M | TU | W | TH | F | SA | SU |
|---|----|----|----|----|----|----|
| | | | | | | 1 |
| 2 | 3 | 4 | 5 | 6 | 7 | 8 |
| 9 | 10 | 11 | 12 | 13 | 14 | 15 |
| 16 | 17 | 18 | 19 | 20 | 21 | 22 |
| 23 | 24 | 25 | 26 | 27 | 28 | 29 |
| 30 | 31 | | | | | |

## CELEBRATIONS/BIRTHDAYS ETC.:

| TASKS | IMPORTANT DATES |
|---|---|
| | |
| | |
| | |
| | |
| | |
| | |
| | |
| | |
| | |
| | |
| | |
| | ● NEW MOON:  8TH AUGUST 2021 |
| | ○ FULL MOON:  22ND AUGUST 2021 |
| | ECLIPSE/SUPERMOON/METEORS |
| | |

## NOTES

# AUGUST 2ND ~ 8TH AUGUST 2021

## IMPORTANT DATES & OBSERVANCES

2ND AUGUST ~ SUMMER BANK HOLIDAY (SCOT.)

**MONDAY**

**TUESDAY**

**WEDNESDAY**

## THURSDAY

## FRIDAY

## SATURDAY

## SUNDAY

# AUGUST 9TH ~ 15TH AUGUST 2021
## IMPORTANT DATES & OBSERVANCES

10TH AUGUST ~ MUHARRAM/ISLAMIC NEW YEAR
15TH AUGUST ~ ASSUMPTION OF MARY

## MONDAY

## TUESDAY

## WEDNESDAY

## THURSDAY

## FRIDAY

## SATURDAY

## SUNDAY

# AUGUST 16TH ~ 22ND AUGUST 2021
## IMPORTANT DATES & OBSERVANCES

19TH AUGUST ~ ASHURA
19TH AUGUST ~ NATIONAL AVIATION DAY (USA)
21ST AUGUST ~ RAKSHA BANDHAN (USA)
21ST AUGUST ~ SENIOR CITIZENS DAY (USA)
22ND AUGUST ~ RAKSHA BANDHAN (UK)

**MONDAY**

**TUESDAY**

**WEDNESDAY**

## THURSDAY

## FRIDAY

## SATURDAY

## SUNDAY

# AUGUST 23RD ~ 29TH AUGUST 2021
## IMPORTANT DATES & OBSERVANCES

26TH AUGUST ~ WOMEN'S EQUALITY DAY (USA)
29TH AUGUST ~ KRISHNA JANMASHTAMI (USA)

## MONDAY

## TUESDAY

## WEDNESDAY

## THURSDAY


## FRIDAY


## SATURDAY


## SUNDAY

# SEPTEMBER

| M | TU | W | TH | F | SA | SU |
|---|----|----|----|----|----|----|
|  |  | 1 | 2 | 3 | 4 | 5 |
| 6 | 7 | 8 | 9 | 10 | 11 | 12 |
| 13 | 14 | 15 | 16 | 17 | 18 | 19 |
| 20 | 21 | 22 | 23 | 24 | 25 | 26 |
| 27 | 28 | 29 | 30 |  |  |  |

## CELEBRATIONS/BIRTHDAYS ETC.:

| TASKS | IMPORTANT DATES |
|---|---|
| | |
| | |
| | |
| | |
| | |
| | |
| | |
| | |
| | |
| | |
| | ⬤ NEW MOON: 7TH SEPTEMBER 2021 |
| | ◯ FULL MOON: 21ST SEPTEMBER 2021 |
| | ECLIPSE/SUPERMOON/METEORS |
| | |

## NOTES

# AUGUST 30TH ~ 7TH SEPTEMBER 2021
## IMPORTANT DATES & OBSERVANCES

30TH AUGUST ~ SUMMER BANK HOLIDAY (UK)
30TH AUGUST ~ KRISHNA JANMASHTAMI (UK)

## MONDAY

## TUESDAY

## WEDNESDAY

## THURSDAY

## FRIDAY

## SATURDAY

## SUNDAY

# SEPTEMBER 6TH ~ 12TH SEPTEMBER 2021
## IMPORTANT DATES & OBSERVANCES

6TH SEPTEMBER ~ LABOR DAY (USA)
7TH SEPTEMBER ~ ROSH HASHANA
9TH SEPTEMBER ~ GANESH CHATURTHI (USA)
10TH SEPTEMBER ~ GANESH CHATURTHI (UK)
11TH SEPTEMBER ~ PATRIOT DAY (USA)
12TH SEPTEMBER ~ NATIONAL GRANDPARENTS DAY (USA)

## MONDAY

## TUESDAY

## WEDNESDAY

## THURSDAY

## FRIDAY

## SATURDAY

## SUNDAY

# SEPTEMBER 13TH ~ 19TH SEPTEMBER 2021
## <u>IMPORTANT DATES & OBSERVANCES</u>
16TH SEPTEMBER ~ YOM KIPPUR
17TH SEPTEMBER ~ CONSTITUTION CITIZENSHIP DAY (USA)

## <u>MONDAY</u>

## <u>TUESDAY</u>

## <u>WEDNESDAY</u>

## THURSDAY

## FRIDAY

## SATURDAY

## SUNDAY

# SEPTEMBER 20TH – 26TH SEPTEMBER 2021

## IMPORTANT DATES & OBSERVANCES

21ST SEPTEMBER ~ SUKKOT
22ND SEPTEMBER ~ AUTUMN/FALL EQUINOX

## MONDAY

## TUESDAY

## WEDNESDAY

## THURSDAY

## FRIDAY

## SATURDAY

## SUNDAY

# SEPTEMBER 27TH ~ 3RD OCTOBER 2021

## IMPORTANT DATES & OBSERVANCES

27TH SEPTEMBER ~ HASHANA RABBAH
28TH SEPTEMBER ~ SHEMINI ATZERET
29TH SEPTEMBER ~ SIMCHAT TORAH

## MONDAY

## TUESDAY

## WEDNESDAY

## THURSDAY

## FRIDAY

## SATURDAY

## SUNDAY

# OCTOBER

| M | TU | W | TH | F | SA | SU |
|---|----|----|----|----|----|----|
|   |    |    |    | 1 | 2 | 3 |
| 4 | 5 | 6 | 7 | 8 | 9 | 10 |
| 11 | 12 | 13 | 14 | 15 | 16 | 17 |
| 18 | 19 | 20 | 21 | 22 | 23 | 24 |
| 25 | 26 | 27 | 28 | 29 | 30 | 31 |

## CELEBRATIONS/BIRTHDAYS ETC.:

| TASKS | IMPORTANT DATES |
|---|---|
|  |  |
|  |  |
|  |  |
|  |  |
|  |  |
|  |  |
|  |  |
|  |  |
|  |  |
|  |  |
|  | ● NEW MOON:  6TH OCTOBER 2021 |
|  | ○ FULL MOON:  20TH OCTOBER 2021 |
|  | ECLIPSE/SUPERMOON/METEORS |
|  |  |

## NOTES

|  |
|---|
|  |
|  |
|  |
|  |
|  |
|  |
|  |
|  |
|  |
|  |
|  |
|  |
|  |
|  |
|  |
|  |

# OCTOBER 4TH ~ 10TH OCTOBER 2021

## IMPORTANT DATES & OBSERVANCES

4TH OCTOBER ~ FEAST OF ST. FRANCIS OF ASSISI
4TH OCTOBER ~ CHILD HEALTH DAY (USA)
6TH OCTOBER ~ NAVARATRI (USA)
7TH OCTOBER ~ NAVARATRI (UK)
9TH OCTOBER ~ LEIF ERIKSON (USA)

## MONDAY

## TUESDAY

## WEDNESDAY

## THURSDAY

## FRIDAY

## SATURDAY

## SUNDAY

# OCTOBER 11TH ~ 17TH OCTOBER 2021
## IMPORTANT DATES & OBSERVANCES

11TH OCTOBER ~ COLUMBUS DAY (USA)
14TH OCTOBER ~ DUSSEHRA
15TH OCTOBER ~ BOSS'S DAY (USA)

## MONDAY

## TUESDAY

## WEDNESDAY

# THURSDAY

# FRIDAY

# SATURDAY

# SUNDAY

# OCTOBER 18TH ~ 24TH OCTOBER 2021

## IMPORTANT DATES & OBSERVANCES

19TH OCTOBER ~ MILAD UN NABI (MAWLID)
19TH OCTOBER ~ THE PROPHET'S BIRTHDAY

## MONDAY

## TUESDAY

## WEDNESDAY

## THURSDAY

## FRIDAY

## SATURDAY

## SUNDAY

# OCTOBER 29TH ~ 31ST OCTOBER 2021

## IMPORTANT DATES & OBSERVANCES

31ST OCTOBER ~ HALLOWEEN/ALL HALLOWS EVE
31ST OCTOBER ~ DAYLIGHT SAVINGS TIME ENDS (UK)

## MONDAY

## TUESDAY

## WEDNESDAY

## THURSDAY

## FRIDAY

## SATURDAY

## SUNDAY

# NOVEMBER

| M | TU | W | TH | F | SA | SU |
|---|----|----|----|----|----|----|
| 1 | 2 | 3 | 4 | 5 | 6 | 7 |
| 8 | 9 | 10 | 11 | 12 | 13 | 14 |
| 15 | 16 | 17 | 18 | 19 | 20 | 21 |
| 22 | 23 | 24 | 25 | 26 | 27 | 28 |
| 29 | 30 | | | | | |

## CELEBRATIONS/BIRTHDAYS ETC.:

| TASKS | IMPORTANT DATES |
|---|---|
| | |
| | |
| | |
| | |
| | |
| | |
| | |
| | |
| | |
| | |
| | ● NEW MOON:  4TH NOVEMBER 2021 |
| | ○ FULL MOON:  19TH NOVEMBER 2021 |
| | ECLIPSE/SUPERMOON/METEORS |
| | 18TH/19TH NOV: PARTIAL SOLAR ECLIPSE |

## NOTES

# NOVEMBER 1ST ~ 7TH NOVEMBER 2021

## IMPORTANT DATES & OBSERVANCES

1ST NOVEMBER ~ ALL SAINTS' DAY
2ND NOVEMBER ~ ALL SOULS DAY
4TH NOVEMBER ~ DIWALI/DEEPAVALI
5TH NOVEMBER ~ FIREWORKS NIGHT/GUY FAWKES DAY (UK)
7TH NOVEMBER ~ DAYLIGHT SAVING TIME ENDS (USA)

## MONDAY

## TUESDAY

## WEDNESDAY

## THURSDAY

## FRIDAY

## SATURDAY

## SUNDAY

# NOVEMBER 8TH ~ 14TH NOVEMBER 2021

## IMPORTANT DATES & OBSERVANCES

11TH NOVEMBER ~ VETERANS DAY (USA)
11TH NOVEMBER ~ REMEMBRANCE DAY (UK)
14TH NOVEMBER ~ REMEMBRANCE SUNDAY (UK)

## MONDAY

## TUESDAY

## WEDNESDAY

## THURSDAY

## FRIDAY

## SATURDAY

## SUNDAY

# NOVEMBER 15TH ~ 21ST NOVEMBER 2021
## IMPORTANT DATES & OBSERVANCES

### MONDAY

### TUESDAY

### WEDNESDAY

## THURSDAY

## FRIDAY

## SATURDAY

## SUNDAY

# NOVEMBER 22ND ~ 28TH NOVEMBER 2021

## IMPORTANT DATES & OBSERVANCES

25TH NOVEMBER ~ THANKSGIVING (USA)
26TH NOVEMBER ~ BLACK FRIDAY (USA)
28TH NOVEMBER ~ ADVENT

## MONDAY

## TUESDAY

## WEDNESDAY

## THURSDAY

## FRIDAY

## SATURDAY

## SUNDAY

# DECEMBER

| M | TU | W | TH | F | SA | SU |
|---|---|---|---|---|---|---|
| | | 1 | 2 | 3 | 4 | 5 |
| 6 | 7 | 8 | 9 | 10 | 11 | 12 |
| 13 | 14 | 15 | 16 | 17 | 18 | 19 |
| 20 | 21 | 22 | 23 | 24 | 25 | 26 |
| 27 | 28 | 29 | 30 | 31 | | |

## CELEBRATIONS/BIRTHDAYS ETC.:

| TASKS | IMPORTANT DATES |
|---|---|
|  |  |
|  |  |
|  |  |
|  |  |
|  |  |
|  |  |
|  |  |
|  |  |
|  |  |
|  |  |
|  |  |
|  | ⬤ NEW MOON: 4TH DECEMBER 2021 |
|  | ◯ FULL MOON: 19TH DECEMBER 2021 |
|  | ECLIPSE/SUPERMOON/METEORS |
|  | 4TH DEC: TOTAL SOLAR ECLIPSE |

## NOTES

# NOVEMBER 29TH ~ 5TH DECEMBER 2021

## IMPORTANT DATES & OBSERVANCES
29TH NOVEMBER ~ CYBER MONDAY (USA)
29TH NOVEMBER ~ FIRST DAY OF CHANUKAH/ HANUKKAH
30TH NOVEMBER ~ ST. ANDREW'S DAY (SCOT.)

## MONDAY

## TUESDAY

## WEDNESDAY

## THURSDAY

## FRIDAY

## SATURDAY

## SUNDAY

# DECEMBER 6TH ~ 12TH DECEMBER 2021

## IMPORTANT DATES & OBSERVANCES

6TH DECEMBER ~ LAST DAY OF HANUKKAH
6TH DECEMBER ~ ST. NICHOLAS DAY (USA)
7TH DECEMBER ~ PEARL HARBOR REMEMBRANCE DAY (USA)
8TH DECEMBER ~ FEAST OF THE IMMACULATE CONCEPTION

## MONDAY

## TUESDAY

## WEDNESDAY

## THURSDAY



## FRIDAY



## SATURDAY



## SUNDAY

# DECEMBER 13TH ~ 19TH DECEMBER 2021

## IMPORTANT DATES & OBSERVANCES
17TH DECEMBER ~ WRIGHT BROTHERS DAY (USA)

**MONDAY**

**TUESDAY**

**WEDNESDAY**

## THURSDAY

## FRIDAY

## SATURDAY

## SUNDAY

# DECEMBER 20TH ~ 26TH DECEMBER 2021

## IMPORTANT DATES & OBSERVANCES

21ST DECEMBER ~ WINTER SOLSTICE
24TH DECEMBER ~ CHRISTMAS EVE
25TH DECEMBER ~ CHRISTMAS DAY
26TH DECEMBER ~ BOXING DAY
26TH DECEMBER ~ KWANZAA DAY UNTIL 1ST JANUARY

## MONDAY

## TUESDAY

## WEDNESDAY

## THURSDAY

## FRIDAY

## SATURDAY

## SUNDAY

# DECEMBER 27TH ~ 2ND JANUARY 2022

## IMPORTANT DATES & OBSERVANCES

27TH DECEMBER ~ CHRISTMAS DAY (SUBSTITUTE DAY) IN (UK)
28TH DECEMBER ~ BOXING DAY  (SUBSTITUTE DAY) IN (UK)
31ST DECEMBER ~ NEW YEARS EVE
1ST JANUARY ~ NEW YEARS DAY

## MONDAY

## TUESDAY

## WEDNESDAY

## THURSDAY

## FRIDAY

## SATURDAY

## SUNDAY

# JANUARY

| M | TU | W | TH | F | SA | SU |
|---|----|----|----|----|----|----|
| 27 | 28 | 29 | 30 | 31 | 1 | ● 2 |
| 3 | 4 | 5 | 6 | 7 | 8 | 9 |
| 10 | 11 | 12 | 13 | 14 | 15 | 16 |
| ○ 17 | 18 | 19 | 20 | 21 | 22 | 23 |
| 24 | 25 | 26 | 27 | 28 | 29 | 30 |
| 31 | | | | | | |

## CELEBRATIONS/BIRTHDAYS ETC.:

| TASKS | IMPORTANT DATES |
|---|---|
| | |
| | |
| | |
| | |
| | |
| | |
| | |
| | |
| | |
| | |
| | ● NEW MOON: 2ND JANUARY 2022 |
| | ○ FULL MOON: 17TH JANUARY 2022 |
| | ECLIPSE/SUPERMOON/METEORS |
| | |

## NOTES

# GARDENER'S

# PLANS & LOGS

| PLANTS THAT ARE PLANTED & TO BE PLANTED | | |
|---|---|---|
| NAME OF PLANT | NAME OF PLANT | NAME OF PLANT |
| | | |
| | | |
| | | |
| | | |
| | | |
| | | |
| | | |
| | | |
| | | |
| | | |
| | | |
| | | |
| | | |
| | | |
| | | |
| | | |
| | | |
| | | |
| | | |
| | | |
| | | |
| | | |
| | | |
| | | |
| | | |
| | | |
| | | |
| | | |
| | | |
| | | |
| | | |
| | | |
| | | |
| | | |

# CROP ROTATION – ALLOTMENT PLANNER

EACH SQUARE = 2CM X 2CM =        FT/MTR

# CROP ROTATION – ALLOTMENT PLANNER

EACH SQUARE = 2CM X 2CM =          FT/MTR

Date:

Name of Plant:

## Watering Requirements

💧　💧💧　💧💧💧

## Sunlight/Shade Requirements

☀ ◑ ●

☐ Seed/Pot ☐ Transplant ☐ Pick/Dead Head ☐ Dry Seed/Hang

| Date | Plant Requirements ... |
|------|------------------------|
|      |                        |
|      |                        |
|      |                        |
|      |                        |
|      |                        |
|      |                        |
|      |                        |

Notes:

Outcome:

Uses:

| Date: |
| Name of Plant: |

## Watering Requirements

💧　💧💧　💧💧💧

## Sunlight/Shade Requirements

☼　◐　●

☐ Seed/Pot　☐ Transplant　☐ Pick/Dead Head　☐ Dry Seed/Hang

| Date | Plant Requirements ... |
|------|------------------------|
|      |                        |
|      |                        |
|      |                        |
|      |                        |
|      |                        |
|      |                        |
|      |                        |

Notes:

Outcome:

Uses:

| Date: |
|---|
| Name of Plant: |

## Watering Requirements

🌢  🌢🌢  🌢🌢🌢

## Sunlight/Shade Requirements

☀ ◑ ●

☐ Seed/Pot  ☐ Transplant  ☐ Pick/Dead Head  ☐ Dry Seed/Hang

| Date | Plant Requirements ... |
|---|---|
|  |  |
|  |  |
|  |  |
|  |  |
|  |  |
|  |  |
|  |  |

| Notes: |
|---|
|  |

| Outcome: |
|---|
|  |

| Uses: |
|---|
|  |

| Date: |
| Name of Plant: |

## Watering Requirements

💧　　💧💧　　💧💧💧

## Sunlight/Shade Requirements

☼ ◑ ●

☐ Seed/Pot　　☐ Transplant　　☐ Pick/Dead Head　　☐ Dry Seed/Hang

| Date | Plant Requirements ... |
| --- | --- |
|  |  |
|  |  |
|  |  |
|  |  |
|  |  |
|  |  |
|  |  |

| Notes: |
| --- |
|  |

| Outcome: |
| --- |
|  |

| Uses: |
| --- |
|  |

| Date: |
|---|
| Name of Plant: |

## Watering Requirements

💧    💧💧    💧💧💧

## Sunlight/Shade Requirements  ☼  ☼  ●

☐ Seed/Pot    ☐ Transplant    ☐ Pick/Dead Head    ☐ Dry Seed/Hang

| Date | Plant Requirements ... |
|---|---|
|  |  |
|  |  |
|  |  |
|  |  |
|  |  |
|  |  |
|  |  |

**Notes:**

**Outcome:**

**Uses:**

| Date: |
|---|
| Name of Plant: |

**Watering Requirements**

💧   💧💧   💧💧💧

**Sunlight/Shade Requirements** ☀ ☼ ⬤

☐ Seed/Pot   ☐ Transplant   ☐ Pick/Dead Head   ☐ Dry Seed/Hang

| Date | Plant Requirements ... |
|---|---|
|  |  |
|  |  |
|  |  |
|  |  |
|  |  |
|  |  |
|  |  |

| Notes: |
|---|
|  |

| Outcome: |
|---|
|  |

| Uses: |
|---|
|  |

| Date: |
|---|
| Name of Plant: |

## Watering Requirements

💧   💧💧   💧💧💧

## Sunlight/Shade Requirements

☀ ☀ ●

☐ Seed/Pot   ☐ Transplant   ☐ Pick/Dead Head   ☐ Dry Seed/Hang

| Date | Plant Requirements ... |
|---|---|
|  |  |
|  |  |
|  |  |
|  |  |
|  |  |
|  |  |
|  |  |

| Notes: |
|---|
|  |

| Outcome: |
|---|
|  |

| Uses: |
|---|
|  |

| Date: |
| --- |
| Name of Plant: |

## Watering Requirements

💧   💧💧   💧💧💧

## Sunlight/Shade Requirements ☀ ◑ ●

☐ Seed/Pot   ☐ Transplant   ☐ Pick/Dead Head   ☐ Dry Seed/Hang

| Date | Plant Requirements ... |
| --- | --- |
|  |  |
|  |  |
|  |  |
|  |  |
|  |  |
|  |  |
|  |  |

| Notes: |
| --- |
|  |

| Outcome: |
| --- |
|  |

| Uses: |
| --- |
|  |

| Date: |
| :--- |
| Name of Plant: |

## Watering Requirements

💧    💧💧    💧💧💧

## Sunlight/Shade Requirements

☀ ☀ ⬤

☐ Seed/Pot    ☐ Transplant    ☐ Pick/Dead Head    ☐ Dry Seed/Hang

| Date | Plant Requirements ... |
| :--- | :--- |
|  |  |
|  |  |
|  |  |
|  |  |
|  |  |
|  |  |
|  |  |

| Notes: |
| :--- |
|  |

| Outcome: |
| :--- |
|  |

| Uses: |
| :--- |
|  |

| Date: |
| Name of Plant: |

## Watering Requirements

💧   💧💧   💧💧💧

## Sunlight/Shade Requirements

☀ ☼ ●

☐ Seed/Pot    ☐ Transplant    ☐ Pick/Dead Head    ☐ Dry Seed/Hang

| Date | Plant Requirements ... |
|------|------------------------|
|      |                        |
|      |                        |
|      |                        |
|      |                        |
|      |                        |
|      |                        |
|      |                        |

**Notes:**

**Outcome:**

**Uses:**

| Date: |
| Name of Plant: |

## Watering Requirements

💧　　💧💧　　💧💧💧

## Sunlight/Shade Requirements  ☀ ◐ ●

☐ Seed/Pot　☐ Transplant　☐ Pick/Dead Head　☐ Dry Seed/Hang

| Date | Plant Requirements ... |
|------|------------------------|
|      |                        |
|      |                        |
|      |                        |
|      |                        |
|      |                        |
|      |                        |
|      |                        |

| Notes: |
|--------|
|        |

| Outcome: |
|----------|
|          |

| Uses: |
|-------|
|       |

Date:

Name of Plant:

## Watering Requirements

💧   💧💧   💧💧💧

## Sunlight/Shade Requirements

☼   ☼   ●

☐ Seed/Pot   ☐ Transplant   ☐ Pick/Dead Head   ☐ Dry Seed/Hang

| Date | Plant Requirements ... |
|------|------------------------|
|      |                        |
|      |                        |
|      |                        |
|      |                        |
|      |                        |
|      |                        |
|      |                        |

Notes:

Outcome:

Uses:

| Date: |
| --- |
| Name of Plant: |

## Watering Requirements

💧   💧💧   💧💧💧

## Sunlight/Shade Requirements ☼ ◐ ●

☐ Seed/Pot   ☐ Transplant   ☐ Pick/Dead Head   ☐ Dry Seed/Hang

| Date | Plant Requirements ... |
| --- | --- |
|  |  |
|  |  |
|  |  |
|  |  |
|  |  |
|  |  |
|  |  |

| Notes: |
| --- |
|  |

| Outcome: |
| --- |
|  |

| Uses: |
| --- |
|  |

| Date: |
|---|
| Name of Plant: |

## Watering Requirements

💧   💧💧   💧💧💧

## Sunlight/Shade Requirements

☼ ☼ ●

☐ Seed/Pot    ☐ Transplant    ☐ Pick/Dead Head    ☐ Dry Seed/Hang

| Date | Plant Requirements ... |
|---|---|
|  |  |
|  |  |
|  |  |
|  |  |
|  |  |
|  |  |
|  |  |

**Notes:**

**Outcome:**

**Uses:**

Date:

Name of Plant:

**Watering Requirements**

💧    💧💧    💧💧💧

**Sunlight/Shade Requirements** ☼ ◐ ●

☐ Seed/Pot    ☐ Transplant    ☐ Pick/Dead Head    ☐ Dry Seed/Hang

| Date | Plant Requirements ... |
|------|------------------------|
|      |                        |
|      |                        |
|      |                        |
|      |                        |
|      |                        |
|      |                        |
|      |                        |

Notes:

Outcome:

Uses:

| Date: |
|---|
| Name of Plant: |

## Watering Requirements
💧     💧💧     💧💧💧

## Sunlight/Shade Requirements ☀ ◑ ●

☐ Seed/Pot    ☐ Transplant    ☐ Pick/Dead Head    ☐ Dry Seed/Hang

| Date | Plant Requirements ... |
|---|---|
|  |  |
|  |  |
|  |  |
|  |  |
|  |  |
|  |  |
|  |  |

| Notes: |
|---|
|  |

| Outcome: |
|---|
|  |

| Uses: |
|---|
|  |

| Date: |
| Name of Plant: |

## Watering Requirements

💧　　💧💧　　　💧💧💧

## Sunlight/Shade Requirements

☼ ◐ ●

☐ Seed/Pot　　☐ Transplant　　☐ Pick/Dead Head　　☐ Dry Seed/Hang

| Date | Plant Requirements ... |
|------|------------------------|
|      |                        |
|      |                        |
|      |                        |
|      |                        |
|      |                        |
|      |                        |
|      |                        |

Notes:

Outcome:

Uses:

| Date: |
| --- |
| Name of Plant: |

## Watering Requirements

💧    💧💧    💧💧💧

## Sunlight/Shade Requirements

☼ ☼ ●

☐ Seed/Pot    ☐ Transplant    ☐ Pick/Dead Head    ☐ Dry Seed/Hang

| Date | Plant Requirements ... |
| --- | --- |
|  |  |
|  |  |
|  |  |
|  |  |
|  |  |
|  |  |
|  |  |

Notes:

Outcome:

Uses:

| Date: |
| Name of Plant: |

## Watering Requirements

💧    💧💧    💧💧💧

## Sunlight/Shade Requirements ☀ ◑ ●

☐ Seed/Pot    ☐ Transplant    ☐ Pick/Dead Head    ☐ Dry Seed/Hang

| Date | Plant Requirements ... |
|------|------------------------|
|      |                        |
|      |                        |
|      |                        |
|      |                        |
|      |                        |
|      |                        |
|      |                        |

| Notes: |
|--------|
|        |

| Outcome: |
|----------|
|          |

| Uses: |
|-------|
|       |

| Date: |
|---|
| Name of Plant: |

## Watering Requirements

💧    💧💧    💧💧💧

## Sunlight/Shade Requirements ☀ ◑ ●

☐ Seed/Pot    ☐ Transplant    ☐ Pick/Dead Head    ☐ Dry Seed/Hang

| Date | Plant Requirements ... |
|---|---|
|  |  |
|  |  |
|  |  |
|  |  |
|  |  |
|  |  |
|  |  |

**Notes:**

**Outcome:**

**Uses:**

| Date: |
|---|
| Name of Plant: |

## Watering Requirements

💧   💧💧   💧💧💧

## Sunlight/Shade Requirements

☼ ◐ ●

☐ Seed/Pot  ☐ Transplant  ☐ Pick/Dead Head  ☐ Dry Seed/Hang

| Date | Plant Requirements ... |
|---|---|
|  |  |
|  |  |
|  |  |
|  |  |
|  |  |
|  |  |
|  |  |

| Notes: |
|---|
|  |

| Outcome: |
|---|
|  |

| Uses: |
|---|
|  |

| Date: |
|---|

| Name of Plant: |
|---|

## Watering Requirements

💧   💧💧   💧💧💧

## Sunlight/Shade Requirements ☀ ◐ ●

☐ Seed/Pot    ☐ Transplant    ☐ Pick/Dead Head    ☐ Dry Seed/Hang

| Date | Plant Requirements ... |
|---|---|
|  |  |
|  |  |
|  |  |
|  |  |
|  |  |
|  |  |
|  |  |

| Notes: |
|---|

| Outcome: |
|---|

| Uses: |
|---|

| Date: |
| --- |
| Name of Plant: |

## Watering Requirements

💧   💧💧   💧💧💧

## Sunlight/Shade Requirements ☀ ◐ ●

☐ Seed/Pot   ☐ Transplant   ☐ Pick/Dead Head   ☐ Dry Seed/Hang

| Date | Plant Requirements ... |
| --- | --- |
|  |  |
|  |  |
|  |  |
|  |  |
|  |  |
|  |  |
|  |  |

| Notes: |
| --- |
|  |

| Outcome: |
| --- |
|  |

| Uses: |
| --- |
|  |

| Date: |
| Name of Plant: |

## Watering Requirements

💧     💧💧     💧💧💧

## Sunlight/Shade Requirements ☀ ◑ ●

☐ Seed/Pot     ☐ Transplant     ☐ Pick/Dead Head     ☐ Dry Seed/Hang

| Date | Plant Requirements ... |
|------|------------------------|
|      |                        |
|      |                        |
|      |                        |
|      |                        |
|      |                        |
|      |                        |
|      |                        |

| Notes: |

| Outcome: |

| Uses: |

| Date: |
| :--- |
| Name of Plant: |

**Watering Requirements**

💧　　💧💧　　💧💧💧

**Sunlight/Shade Requirements** ☼ ◑ ●

☐ Seed/Pot　　☐ Transplant　　☐ Pick/Dead Head　　☐ Dry Seed/Hang

| Date | Plant Requirements ... |
| :--- | :--- |
|  |  |
|  |  |
|  |  |
|  |  |
|  |  |
|  |  |
|  |  |

| Notes: |
| :--- |
|  |

| Outcome: |
| :--- |
|  |

| Uses: |
| :--- |
|  |

| Date: |
|---|
| Name of Plant: |

## Watering Requirements

💧    💧💧     💧💧💧

## Sunlight/Shade Requirements ☀ ◐ ●

☐ Seed/Pot    ☐ Transplant    ☐ Pick/Dead Head    ☐ Dry Seed/Hang

| Date | Plant Requirements ... |
|---|---|
|  |  |
|  |  |
|  |  |
|  |  |
|  |  |
|  |  |
|  |  |

| Notes: |
|---|
|  |

| Outcome: |
|---|
|  |

| Uses: |
|---|
|  |

| Date: |
| Name of Plant: |

## Watering Requirements

💧   💧💧   💧💧💧

## Sunlight/Shade Requirements ☀ ◐ ●

☐ Seed/Pot   ☐ Transplant   ☐ Pick/Dead Head   ☐ Dry Seed/Hang

| Date | Plant Requirements ... |
|------|------------------------|
|      |                        |
|      |                        |
|      |                        |
|      |                        |
|      |                        |
|      |                        |
|      |                        |

| Notes: |

| Outcome: |

| Uses: |

| Date: |
| :--- |
| Name of Plant: |

## Watering Requirements

💧    💧💧    💧💧💧

## Sunlight/Shade Requirements ☀ ◐ ●

☐ Seed/Pot    ☐ Transplant    ☐ Pick/Dead Head    ☐ Dry Seed/Hang

| Date | Plant Requirements ... |
| :--- | :--- |
|  |  |
|  |  |
|  |  |
|  |  |
|  |  |
|  |  |
|  |  |

| Notes: |
| :--- |
|  |

| Outcome: |
| :--- |
|  |

| Uses: |
| :--- |
|  |

# NOTES

# NOTES

# NOTES

| CONTACTS NAME | TELEPHONE NUMBER |
|---|---|
| | |
| | |
| | |
| | |
| | |
| | |
| | |
| | |
| | |
| | |
| | |
| | |
| | |
| | |
| | |
| | |
| | |
| | |
| | |
| | |
| | |
| | |
| | |
| | |
| | |
| | |
| | |
| | |
| | |
| | |
| | |
| | |
| | |
| | |
| | |

| CONTACTS NAME | TELEPHONE NUMBER |
|---|---|
| | |
| | |
| | |
| | |
| | |
| | |
| | |
| | |
| | |
| | |
| | |
| | |
| | |
| | |
| | |
| | |
| | |
| | |
| | |
| | |
| | |
| | |
| | |
| | |
| | |
| | |
| | |
| | |
| | |
| | |
| | |
| | |
| | |
| | |
| | |
| | |
| | |
| | |

Printed in Great Britain
by Amazon